THE PERENNIAL WORKFORCE

BABY BOOMERS BLOOMING AND MAKING MONEY AFTER RETIREMENT

by

Marva L. Goldsmith

marva@marvagoldsmith.com

ISBN-13: 978-0692909744
ISBN-10: 0692909745

Foreword

Marva asked me to write the foreword for her book because as of December 31, 2016, I am retired! My vision of retirement is like my mother's vision when she retired at 51 years old. She has now been retired for the same amount of time that she worked – 32 years! Within a year of retirement, she moved to the Pacific Northwest and without much fanfare, devoted her life to public service.

Here's the beauty of life: when a seed is planted, you must water it and watch it grow. My sister, Marva, son, Charles, and I attended an online class with life coach, Brendon Burchard, to kick off the new year in 2016. It planted a seed for each of us to water. For me, it was envisioning retirement; for Marva, it was moving to a walkable community; and for Charles, it was pursuing his passion for developing young people through his work and community service. Happily, each of us have accomplished our goals.

I created my Retirement Mind Map (see page 91). It has four quadrants: **Passion, Travel, Social Networking, and Volunteerism.**

So now I am armed with a plan, a direction, and a pretty picture (my mind map). Ninety days into retirement and what does it feel like? Great! No alarm clocks or commitments. Well, not exactly, but it's still great.

Here's how things have panned out. In the first month, I took on major renovation projects to create my dream environment. After 90 days, my little dollhouse is almost complete and I look forward to being dust and contractor-free.

PASSION: I'm passionate about encouraging women (especially minority women) to pursue careers in science, technology, engineering, and math (STEM). I'm an engineer and recognize the grounding that I received in engineering school at Michigan State University as well as in my career; I also recognize the importance of sharing that knowledge. While things have not gone exactly as planned, I have had the opportunity to mentor high school girls about STEM careers. For my first assignment, I was asked to design a workshop about managing time to study at the Detroit Delta Prep Academy. Planning and organizing is in my DNA, so I figured, how hard can this be? I worked on my PowerPoint (a residual response from working in corporate America for more than 30 years). It was not germane to the story until now. I bored the aspiring STEM potentials to tears. So, I did what any good facilitator does and surveyed my 25 ninth graders. Their desire was for me to bring them food and to help them learn 'how to act and dress.' That translated into brand and image. (I hit the EASY button and called Marva). I returned, armed with creativity, fun, and what they desired to see. We had a great time learning together.

VOLUNTEERISM: I volunteer at the Michigan Science Center and have begun training to deliver eight free science and engineering workshops to a group of youth. Aside from my favorite charities: my beloved sorority, my church, and the Charles Wright African American Museum, I am also involved in grass roots organizations that are on the plan. Volunteerism gives me great emotional satisfaction. I built my retirement mind map based on volunteering my time through established organizations. I know now that volunteerism comes in many forms, including a cause or two that inspire me and stokes my passion. I just hope that I can make a difference.

THE SOCIAL NETWORK/TRAVEL: In the first 90 days of my retirement, I traveled to the Grand Bahamas, Cancun, and Tacoma and cancelled a trip to Asia to pay for my 'dollhouse.' I have taken golf lessons in preparation for the spring leagues and joined a fitness club to stay healthy. My social network will also include a Bid Whist club with my old friends just as soon as the 'dollhouse' is complete.

So, what's the point? Whether you are retiring or not, you need a plan. This book is a planning tool that will encourage you to think outside of any self-imposed restrictions.

I'm excited for the future: yours and mine!

Marcia A. Jackson

Acknowledgements

Perhaps this is my second mid-life crisis. *Scratch that:* it's not a crisis – it's an adventure. My first **mid-life adventure** began when I sold my townhouse in the Eastern Market area of Detroit, MI in 2000 -- I took a sabbatical from the company that I had worked for since the age of 17 and attended Harvard University to matriculate with other mid-careerists at the Kennedy School of Government (KSG). I returned briefly after KSG to a corporate downsizing, to which I said a resounding 'yes' to a voluntary separation. The adventure launched a move from Detroit to DC (10 days after 9-11), and a new business and career direction (from the utility sector to image and brand management). My second mid-life adventure started the same way: I sold my townhouse and down-sized from more than 1800 square feet of living space in a Maryland suburb to a 1267 square-foot apartment in the millennial-rich Navy Yard area of Washington, DC.

While right-sizing, I found course materials from engineering school at Michigan State University (now that's been boxed away for quite a while), taxes that dated back to the 1990s, clothing that bore an 'S' that did not stand for Superman, and memorabilia that represented memories for which I could no longer remember the significance of the event that compelled me to covet the token of days gone by. As I prepare for this adventure, I am contemplating the excitement of what's next. It is the same question many Boomers wrestle with whether you call it an encore career, reinvention, re-careering, or just getting a fresh perspective. The quest is the same: **work that sets your soul on fire!**

My mom and sister (Marcia) have set a high bar for what retirement can look like: a blissful life without the need for alarm clocks to wake the body for a work-related event. Both Mom and Marcia volunteer for various causes, providing their time and talents. As I write this action guide, I know that retirement is not in my vernacular. For me, the "R" word is simply reinvention -- revolution -- time to shake things up do something different, perhaps radically different. For those Baby Boomers, who like me are in a continuous state of blooming, looking to re-engage by trading wisdom, time, talent, and sheer tenacity for your own natural energy yield, perhaps this experience is for you. Hence, the title, *The Perennial Workforce: Baby Boomers Blooming and Making Money After Retirement.* In nature, perennials are enduring or continually recurring. Most notably as plant life, perennials tend to come back heartier and livelier than in the last season. This action guide is for Boomers who are looking for their next adventure, heartier than the last season and ready to bloom. Throughout the book, you will find stories of members of the perennial workforce whose careers have come back to life and are flourishing.

I encourage you to read this action guide with a pen in hand (that's why I call it an action guide. Its purpose is for you to read, plan, and act). If you are scarred by the notion of writing in a book, grab a piece of paper – this is not a passive read. We are co-creating this experience together. As my collaborator, you are also embarking on your own next adventure, and indeed you are prominently featured in mine.

As I moved into my shiny new Navy Yard apartment, I took a 360 turn and threw my (imaginary) hat up in the air – *a nod to Mary Tyler Moore* … and my fellow Boomers – an acknowledgement of the start of this new adventure!

Acknowledging first the Divine Source of this creation – I pray that all who read this action guide will receive a blessing – a new idea that will launch a powerful and prosperous adventure filled with energy and joy; and to my mom and sister who provide me daily inspiration.

Many thanks to all who have contributed to this action guide by providing ideas, edits, and kind words of encouragement, including contributors: Marcia Jackson, Abby Locke, Satori Shakoor, Wendy Leigh, Carla Dancy Smith, Deborah Chin, and Hebah Saddique; reviewers: Katherine Gekker, Gwen Kelly, Robin Fenner, Darnell Mitchell, Rita Clark, Margo Lovett, Vernell Sims, and Patricia Quarles; and a host of Facebook friends and LinkedIn connections (too numerous to name) who chimed in to help me name the book: special thanks to Barbara Beizer (who suggested the idea of *perennials*).

THE PERENNIAL WORKFORCE
Baby Boomers Blooming
And Making Money After Retirement

Introduction

Retirement sneaks up on you like the proverbial
"thief in the night!"

First things, first…I'm an average Joe(ann). I grew up on the east side of Detroit with a single mom (my parents divorced when I was a young child), an older sister, and grandmother who lived across the street. I was fortunate to have a nurturing mother, supportive family, and an intellect that launched my engineering career. Working for 20 years at a utility company enabled me to live a comfortable middle-class lifestyle. My point is, if you look in the middle of the bell curve – there I am, peering out wondering how I became close to 60 and not able or ready to retire. Yes, while enjoying the challenge of entrepreneurship, life happened and here I am. I do not have the millions of dollars needed to retire with ease. I work every day to pay the bills, including a $763/month health care premium (for just me). Although I am comfortable and happy, I realize that any twist can change how I live – and at this age, that's an uncomfortable prospect. This guide has everything to do with ideas, choices, and **action**.

It was New Year's Eve. My sister, Marcia, had 10 minutes to make a life-altering decision. Thirty-six years of service suddenly boiled down to a 10-minute period in which she had to decide. She had been planning for months now – attended retirement classes – hired a financial planner – and now it was time to decide.

Marcia was not alone on that New Year's Eve. Thousands of others make the decision every day to retire or not? In those final minutes, they stare at the company's benefits page wondering if the pension will be enough.

The decision: Do you hit the button to resend the offer and return to work as if the retirement party never happened?

Should you return all the nice gifts and cards provided by well-wishers? Or, do you take the plunge that so many of your gray-haired buddies have already taken? *Eight minutes to decide.*

So, let's take a quick assessment.

Have you:

- ✓ Made calculations to ensure that the bills can be paid? **Check**. *But, I want more than to just pay the bills.*
- ✓ Got stable investments for a rainy day? **Check**. *But, what if it's more than a rainy day? What if it's a hurricane?*
- ✓ Allocated sufficient money in the monthly budget for a good meal or two in a nice restaurant? **Check**. *Five minutes left.*
- ✓ Have money to travel and tick off those bucket list destinations? **Check**. *I want money to travel every now and then – after all, I'm retired!*

Two minutes. Decide. Hit the button to resend the retirement? As Oprah would say, "Here's what I know for sure…"

If, what you know for sure is that:

- You are leaving behind a daily routine from which you earned a living.
- You are grateful for the work, the company, your pension, and the people that you met.
- You are ready for new opportunities to create, share, and enjoy.

Then, you are ready to start the next stage of life – *a new adventure!*

If you're reading this book, you're either retired and looking for work, or contemplating retirement and considering work after retirement.

Before you turn the page, grab a pen and prepare to read **and write**. By the time you have completed this action guide, you will emerge with a plan of action to carve out the next steps on your journey.

Identify the lessons learned from past challenges and contemplate what you're leaving behind.

LESSONS LEARNED:	I AM LEAVING BEHIND:

Celebrate your successes. **Visualize what the future holds for you.**

BIGGEST SUCCESSES:	I AM MOVING TOWARDS:

CHAPTER 1:

Work After Retirement: My Options?

You picked up this book for a reason. Let's explore why you **need**, no let's say **want,** to go back to work before you begin looking for a job. *'Need' suggests a sense of desperation that may lead to finding work that is minimally acceptable.* However, if you are looking for work to pay the bills (refer to Chapter 3: I Create for the Basics), certainly take care of your immediate needs, but don't allow emotionally-driven desperation to determine how and where you work, especially after retirement.

In other words, if this is your second bite at the apple, **find the biggest, juiciest apple that you can, and take a big satisfying bite!**

For example, if you have applied to become a Walmart Greeter, be clear that the reason you are greeting Walmart customers is because you enjoy meeting people, Walmart has good benefits and you love to shop at Walmart – so this is a **WIN-WIN** opportunity. You are not planning to work at Walmart because it's the only job that you *think* you will be able to find. There's a different energy in how you are positioning yourself to attract the type of work that you will enjoy.

Let's make an assumption: work after retirement (especially if it's been 20, 30 or 40 years) should not *feel* like WORK, in the sense it is a mental or physical activity as a means of earning income (Webster's definition) – even the definition lacks luster, joy and energy.

At this point in our journey, work should simply be **an extension of who you are that is in harmony with your purpose and need for joyful expression.** *(I think my definition is better!)*

69% of Baby Boomers Plan to Find Work After Retirement

A study conducted by the U.S. Census Bureau (based on the 2010 Census) discovered that 69% of Baby Boomers planned to work well after retirement. After doing a bit of research of my own, I found that the most common reasons for a return to work are as follows (please put a checkmark by all that apply):

- ☐ **Lack of Retirement Funds** - More than anything, people are driven by necessity. The stock market and housing market have affected retirement accounts for many Boomers and their window is closing rapidly to build up significant retirement funds.

- ☐ **Lifestyle Maintenance** – Some Boomers don't want to downgrade their style of living: size of home and car, or number and quality of vacations. In fact, since many are still in good health, they want to go on *more* vacations, drive the sports car they've always wanted, or purchase a second home in their favorite vacation location *(and why not?)*

- ☐ **Living on Debt Mountain** – It's not a complete surprise that many retirement accounts have not rebounded since the 2008 recession. However, many big purchases were made when these retirement accounts were booming and debt was not an issue that could alter retirement plans. And since that debt was based on peak earnings, repayment ability has changed post-2008 recession.

☐ **Picture of Health** – People are not only living longer these days, but many are living in better health. The good news is Boomers are physically able to work longer. As a matter of pride, most people want to be productive for as long as possible. So, you can expect good health to play a major role in Boomers' ability to work longer.

☐ **Preserving Your Legacy** – There is a group of Boomers that don't have to work in retirement, but are choosing to do so because they want to leave more to their kids and grandkids. They want to give the next generation a head start and are working or starting a business in their retirement years. In addition, thought leaders have been incentivized to stay on past retirement to continue building their legacy within the organization. Note: this is not the purpose of this book.

☐ **Entrepreneurship** – Another growing trend amongst Boomers is the idea of becoming an entrepreneur. Many Boomers have diligently worked their jobs for the last 30 years or so, and have wanted to venture out into their own business. For one reason or another they never did, and now they have the time, health, and a little money to start a company, buy a franchise, or buy out an existing company. This reminds me of the adage, *"Do what you LOVE and the money will follow."*

There are many ways to earn money without having a full-time job. Did you know that the federal government allows retirees to earn a specific amount and still draw social security? For 2017, that amount is $16,920 **if you are under full retirement age for the entire year,** and $44,880 **in the year you reach full retirement age**. That number represents an opportunity … so don't leave a penny on the table!

There's a paradigm shift occurring as more and more Baby Boomers lose interest in the traditional concept of retirement. There are 75 million Baby Boomers in the United States and 1.1 billion world-wide – 10,000 of which turn 65 every day[1]. Some may have left a position or company after

---

[1] http://www.pewresearch.org/fact-tank/2010/12/29/baby-boomers-retire

a 20 or 30-year contribution, but do not plan to stop working – or contributing. In fact, one friend refers to retirement as the 'R word.' Encore careering is not a new concept (coined by Mark Freedman – www.encore.org). It has also been called re-careering and reinvention. AARP, of course, has been a leader in helping to steer people through their career reinvention journeys. We will define it as meaningful work that you engage in for a purpose that may:

- Cover your daily expenses

- Provide spending money for entertainment

- Build up your emergency fund

- Provide income to meet savings goals

- Stretch your budget

- Help to keep you active and involved

I'm Not Going!

If you're a Baby Boomer, you likely remember Jennifer Holliday or have heard of Jennifer Hudson. Both singers were made famous by the goose-pimple producing song *I'm Telling You, I'm Not Going!* from the movie Dream Girls.[2] It seems that Baby Boomers are singing the same tune as **they just aren't going** either! Let's explore the options if you don't want to, or can't, hang up those work boots.

Unfortunately for many people, the economy, and/or bad planning has wreaked such havoc with their finances that some Boomers have discovered that they can't afford to rely on a pension. Ten percent of workers aged 60+ who took part in a recent survey for CareerBuilder said that they didn't think they would *ever* be able to retire. For them, working after retirement isn't an option - **it's a necessity.**

---

[2] Jennifer Holliday won a Tony Award in the 1981 Broadway Show, *Dream Girls*, and Jennifer Hudson won an Emmy for her role in the 2006 film adaptation.

Considerations for Your Next Step

The ultimate goal would be to find a career that you love, and that has a flexible schedule and earnings potential. Earning money from a craft or passion is ideal. However, income requirements will dictate what kind of job you need. If you need money to pay the mortgage and buy the groceries, then a consistent pay check is more likely what you should seek. If you only want to earn extra cash for spending and having fun, then a more flexible position or prospect is perfect.

Here are a few other considerations:

- The amount of money you need to make
- The amount of time you are willing to dedicate to working
- Your goals and ambitions

Freelance jobs, consulting, on-call, and even part-time jobs are all viable opportunities to help meet your needs without working full-time. In a recent LiveCareer.com article, the idea of portfolio careers is defined as multiple part-time jobs (including temporary jobs, freelancing, and self-employment) with different employers that when combined are the equivalent of a full-time position.

If you are leaving a company that you enjoyed, consider returning. ***What? Return?*** There is an emergence of employers who encourage consulting positions or on-call options for sick days and vacation coverage. These arrangements can offer benefits for both you and your former employer.

So - what are your options?

OPTION 1: Find a Job

Most people retire for a reason: they no longer want to work full-time. Working part-time is an option that provides the best of both worlds. But, don't be afraid to think differently about how you approach part-time work. For example, if you are an early riser, consider applying for jobs that need early morning staff coverage a few days a week. Then, if you need more work, find another position that starts later in the day or other days of the week. Who said you must stick with just one job? The **reality** is that for the more seasoned worker, you may have to start with a part-time position to prove your value – some employers are not as inclined to hire more experienced (translates to more expensive) workers full-time because of the associated cost for benefits. On the bright side, variety may be what you were missing in your old nine-to-five.

Let's explore some potential employment opportunities. Where should you look? Of course, there's the usual places in your community (e.g. utility companies, insurance, retail).

Name them here:

Identify seasonal work in your community:

Consider consulting where you have worked in the last 20 - 30 years:

Identify competitors or organizations that inspire you:

Identify where you can teach your skills – think knowledge transfer:

Identify opportunities to become a consultant for local, county, state or federal government:

Consider perusing Fedbizopps.gov and/or similar state and municipal websites that publish contract awards. These contractors have just been awarded new contracts *(ka-ching)* and may be hiring someone with your skills and experience. Search the database with keywords that define your strengths or capabilities (e.g. process improvement), or include a title that interests you (e.g. project manager). When you find a match, send an email to the human resources officer and the department head (with delivery receipt – you want to know when the email is opened). Congratulate them on their recent award and provide evidence of how your talents and experience can help them address the needs of their new client. If you do not receive a response, follow up with a hard copy via mail service.

You may be wondering; how will I find the names of the head of HR or the hiring manager for this company? Start with LinkedIn if they are not listed on their website. Most likely there is someone within your family of connections that works for the prospect and can provide the information to you. Note: LinkedIn is a valuable resource. If you are not actively building a network of connections, start now!

Be creative. Now that we've started listing the usual suspects, let's have some fun and list dream jobs that won't feel like <u>work</u> – because you're having TOO much fun.

For example, in 2016, I went to Nassau with my sister, Marcia, and friends for a weeklong vacation. Marcia was celebrating her 60th birthday and retirement. Every morning, I'd wake up early, give thanks for another glorious day, and head to the best spot to gain Internet access. I would work for a few hours before the days' beach activities began. One day it occurred to me: *I could work from Nassau.* Did I mention it was December? I envisioned myself, nestled away on Paradise Island with a cool breeze drifting through the veranda. While sipping on tea, I would complete the first conference call for the day. Who said that work must be painful or stressful? In fact, let's find a different word to use to adjust how we feel about this next stage of "**work.**" I think we should replace the word work with "**create.**" Let's engage in the activity of **creation!**

We are creating something new for the world that is both fulfilling and income generating. So, if you decide that your new creative expression will be as a Walmart greeter, and you're in alignment with the idea of creation, you're not just working for Walmart, you are creating a welcoming experience for Walmart shoppers. So, I plan a return to Nassau (or some equally delicious tropical island) next year to create during the entire month of February. If it feels right, I will create from a tropical island during the months of January *and* February every year, returning home just in time for Spring. I can imagine the warmth from the sun kissing my skin every morning from my ocean view as I welcome the new day while I earn a living. Not that I'm ungrateful, but it will provide a completely new perspective than what is offered from the office window that I am peering out of on this wintry February morning.

What about you? <u>Where</u> can you create that will add new life to the idea of a nine-to-five job? <u>How</u> can you create so that the hours are not being counted, but enjoyed?

Close your eyes for **five minutes** and meditate on this idea.

- What are you doing?
- What does it look like?
- More importantly, how does it *feel*?

Seriously, close your eyes … for five minutes. Set a timer. Give me five minutes.

What did you discover? Write down every idea that comes to your mind. Do not judge, just write.

Here are some ideas to get you started:

Cruise ship staff	Recreation director	House sitter (check out https://www.trustedhousesitters.com)

Vision for my new way to create:

What are you doing?	How are you creating?	Where are you creating?

Still hearing crickets? *Check out 101 Weird Ways to Make Money: Cricket Farming, Repossessing Cars, and Other Jobs with Big Upscale and Not Much Competition.* The book is written by Steve Gillman (available on Amazon and Audible.com).

OPTION 2: Startmyownbusiness.com

But, I'm too old to start a business. **Did you say that?** There are opportunities everywhere to create! In 2015, the Kauffman Index of Entrepreneurial Activity reported that almost a quarter of new businesses were started by entrepreneurs aged 55 to 64, a spike from 14 percent in 1996.

Remember **Colonel Sanders**? Everyone knows his story. But, it's a story that I never tire of hearing. Colonel Harland Sanders started cooking at age seven to help feed his younger siblings while his mother worked. The 7th grade dropout left home at age 15 and worked a variety of jobs until age 40, when he acquired a service station in Corbin, Kentucky. He earned a reputation for serving classic Southern dishes to travelers in the back of the service station. In the late 1930's, after he was listed in Duncan Hines' "Adventures in Good Eating," he converted the service station to a full-fledged restaurant.

At the age of sixty-five, he sold the restaurant and lived off savings and a $105 monthly social security check. Almost penniless, the Colonel began selling his "finger lickin' good" fried chicken recipe to restaurants and by 1964, 600 franchises were selling his trademark chicken.

At 73, he sold KFC for $2 million, retained a seat on the Board of Directors and remains the face of the KFC brand. Not bad for a senior citizen!

<u>Colonel Sanders created a business based on his talent for cooking.</u>

What are your talents? List ideas for turning these talents into a business:

MY TALENTS	How can I turn this talent into a business?

Ever heard of Leo and Lillian Goodwin? Leo Goodwin was an accountant who in 1936, at the age of 50, founded GEICO (Government Employee's Insurance Company) in Washington, D.C. by creating an insurance company that "cut out the middle man" and sold policies directly to customers, saving all the money that traditionally went to brokers. Initially GEICO targeted federal employees and some enlisted military officers. Lillian Goodwin provided the administrative role for the fledgling company including marketing, accounting, setting rates, and underwriting. Within a year, GEICO had written 3,700 policies and hired 12 staff members. Today, GEICO employs over 27,000 people and has over 14 million policyholders *–including yours truly.*

<u>The Goodwins created a business based on an observation that insurance costs can be reduced by directly servicing consumers.</u>

Many products and services are developed based on a perceived improvement. It may be a modification to an existing product or service, or something that is a new way of approaching work or play. What observations have you made about the services that you receive? Are there ways to reduce costs, or improve the delivery of those services?

Service received that needs improvement:	How can this service be improved?	How can I turn this idea into a business?

At age 52, Carol Gardner was divorced, broke, and depressed. Her therapist recommended that she get a dog. Later, a friend told her about a Christmas card contest sponsored by a local pet store. Using her background as a creative director in advertising, Carol borrowed a Santa hat from a neighbor, and placed Zelda the dog into a tub filled with bubble bath. She made Zelda a beard from the bubbles and submitted the photo with the quip: "For Christmas I got a dog for my husband ... good trade, huh?" Carol won 40 pounds of free dog food every month for a year.

She sent the prize-winning image out as holiday cards. A few years later, Carol garnered the attention of Hallmark and created an international greeting card, gift, clothing, jewelry and book line that offers wisdom such as "Life is tough ... wear a helmet," "Smile ... it could be worse!" and "Enjoy life ... this is not a rehearsal." Carol tapped into emotions that other people were feeling.

In 2010, Carol's company, Zelda Wisdom was valued at nearly $50 million (latest statistic that I could find). Zelda has been featured on CBS Sunday Morning, NBC Nightly News, Parade Magazine, and USA Today.

<u>Gardner created a business based on her experience – and turned lemons into *sweet* lemonade.</u> She channeled her depression into a lucrative opportunity.

What experiences have you had that might offer wisdom, solutions, and/or laughter to others faced with difficult situations? Before you answer the question, meet my friend, **Satori Shakoor**.

I am so inspired by her story and what she created. Without a doubt, her story will get your creative juices flowing. On the next page, please enjoy this excerpt from a TedX talk that she delivered in Detroit. You can find the full version of her TedX talks on YouTube. Also, visit her website for more inspiring stories with a twist: http://www.twistedtellers.org

Meet Satori

It's 2011, I'm sitting on my couch, holding my breath, waiting for Congress to vote to extend my unemployment benefits. I had been unemployed on and off since 2009. It had been rough as evidenced by the boxes that surrounded me as I prepared to move from my loft into a bedroom in my sister's house.

When I heard myself screaming at the TV and pointing my fingers at a Congress that could care less and couldn't hear me, I vowed that I would never let anyone dictate my life, my liberty, and the pursuit of my happiness. I vowed that I would do what I love to do for the rest of my life no matter what! Yes, I was terrified of my uncertain future when I moved into my sister's bedroom.

But little did I know only a few months later my life would change when I met The Moth at a story slam in Detroit. I love stories. I'm a storyteller and I come from a long line of storytellers who could make going to the corner store sound like Lord of the Rings. The Moth asked me to host the new story slam coming to Ann Arbor, and I said, "I would love to!" It was a love fest. They flew me around the country opening story slams. I hosted the season opener in New York and shared the stage at the Hudson Theater with Adam Gopnik, Richard Price, and Garrison Keillor. My story was on The Moth radio hour, NPR, podcast; people all over the world were thanking me for telling my story—like it was a service.

Then, one night I'm telling my story in front of a sold-out crowd of 900 people in Boston. It had taken six years to crawl back from the devastating grief over the loss of my mother to ovarian cancer in 2005, and then nine months later my son died of a massive seizure, the result of a brain injury he suffered in a car accident just a few years earlier. I was a dead woman walking. My future looked like a joyless chore to live ... and, then I noticed I could hear a pin drop. The audience was breathing with me, leaning forward, waiting for my next word and I was struck by the fact that I had never been listened to so profoundly or heard so deeply; and in the space of my telling and their listening the connection was so powerful that I felt anything was possible. I felt loved. I felt complete. I felt whole and free, healed! When I finished telling my story, they applauded my struggle and my journey of overcoming. I thought every human being on earth no matter who they are should have this experience of being listened to and heard and that's when I knew this is what I'm supposed to do – **this is my calling, my purpose.**

By now I had moved into the basement of a friend's home in Ferndale. I'm sitting in her garden one morning, and I'm thinking if storytelling healed me, couldn't it heal the city of Detroit, because Detroit was grieving, had been grieving for years, had lost many lives, and health, and wealth, and loss of integrity, loss of freedom, of democracy. When I heard the news report that only 17 percent of Detroiters turned out to vote in today's election, I tried to remember did I vote the year my mother and son passed away; as I recall, I could barely get out of bed, and that's when it came to me: the idea for the Secret Society of Twisted Storytellers.

I would use storytelling with the intention of healing, with the intention of connecting the city of Detroit, with the intention of uplifting the spirits of the people who live here, and out of telling stories we would heal and transform, become leaders and take our leadership and transformation into the community and make a difference. I fell in love with the idea, but I didn't have any money. I was living in a friend's basement, but the idea was so delicious that I sold tickets in advance for 15 dollars to my friends and family. I rented this funky little theater space with 45 seats in downtown Detroit. It was a sellout and the four storytellers that evening got a standing ovation. I beamed like a proud mother wondering, *"could this little social experiment work?"*

We did pop ups for eight months until we found a home at the 317-seat auditorium in the Charles Wright Museum of African American History. In 2013, we won the Knight Art Challenge Grant and began to think bigger. *If storytelling could connect, heal, and transform Detroit, could it do the same for the world?*

Twisted Storytellers became a non-profit 501(c)3 with a global mission to connect humanity, heal and transform community, and to provide an uplifting, thought provoking, soul cleansing entertainment experience through the art and craft of storytelling, one story at a time. Since opening in 2012, The Secret Society of Twisted Storytellers has hosted more than 250 storytellers. Among the storytellers that have been featured are George Clinton (to a sold-out crowd of 1050 at the Detroit Institute of Arts); Dick Gregory; Poet Laureate, Naomi Long Madgett; Metallurgist, Carlos Bielbock; Rabbi Yisrael Pinson; and Dr. George Faison. For more information and to hear some of the stories, please visit http://twistedtellers.org.

Identify experiences that you have had that might offer wisdom, solutions, and/or laughter to others faced with difficult situations:

EXPERIENCE	WHAT VALUE CAN YOU PROVIDE OTHERS?	HOW CAN I TURN THIS IDEA INTO A BUSINESS?

A third option: HELP GROW A LOCAL BUSINESS

Helping a small business grow is a very viable option if you do not want a full-time job or the responsibility of starting up a new business. Many startup businesses are small boutique firms, with one to five partners and/or employees. Similar to the business that I started in 2001, entrepreneurs hire freelancers to 'plug the holes' while growing fledgling businesses.

Hebah Saddique has grown her business by helping others grow their small businesses. She is the founder and business strategist for ConsultDC, a strategic planning consulting practice (weconsultdc.com). The following is her advice for working with startup businesses that can benefit from your expertise.

Have you noticed a new company in your community? Whether it's a juice bar, a yoga studio, a skincare company, a social enterprise, a technology company, or a nonprofit organization, all startups need structure, organization, and assistance. Finding one with a mission that aligns with your personal values can be a rewarding fit for both you and the organization.

It's in a startup's nature to be strapped for resources, though that doesn't mean they don't have budget to pay you. Early launching startups are looking for the lowest price, while emerging and growing companies are searching for the best value they can get for their money, and are understandably much more particular and selective in their partnerships.

As a freelancer, you can decide how involved you want to be, and the amount of time you want to spend working with each client. Based on that decision, design your services to reflect the deliverables and price. You can spot opportunities in your own community or network. Services you offer could address a one-time need, (such as working on a project), or provide services on an ongoing basis (such as coaching or bookkeeping). If you made a living for the past 30-40 years as an engineer, yet you happen to also be gifted in writing, consider writing training material for a technology startup. The opportunities are endless.

In considering the theory of "work smarter, not harder," here are a few examples of using your skills to solve challenges typically faced by startup organizations:

Writing: Articulating ideas and communicating points concisely is a treasure and a need in any organization.

- Website content: Refining and editing website copy to articulate the startup's message in appealing and engaging language.

- Blogs and articles: Businesses seek contributing writers who can consistently provide them with material.

Sales: Selling skills are in high demand. If you are an influencer in your network, or have experience closing sales, there are extensive opportunities in the saturated startup market.

- Commission-based sales

- Manage and direct a sales team to deliver results

Organization: Many entrepreneurs tend to value someone who can help them get organized. This extends to both physical spaces and objects, as well as ideas and time.

- Startups need someone to set up systems that they (and their teams) can follow (e.g. filing systems, organization of documents).

- Organizing ideas, team building, and strategic planning sessions.

- Time management, prioritization, and ways to 'get things done.'

Job posts for **part-time** positions can be found on websites such as startuphire.com, flexjobs.com, and Angel List (angel.co).

Three tips for working at a small business or startup:

1. Agree with the number of hours per week - minimum and maximum.

2. Understand in advance how many hats you are expected to wear and what they are.

3. Be flexible.

WHO? – WHY? – WHAT? – HOW? – WHEN? – WHERE?

After pondering the ideas presented in this section for lending your expertise to grow startup businesses, create a plan of action to include:

WHO - Who are your target customers? Name 3 -5 customer groups that could benefit from your expertise. Describe each of them.

> *e.g. Solopreneurs/small partnerships that do not have a salesforce in your industry; nonprofit organizations that need a grant writer; boutique firms with new contracts that do not have in-house accounting.*

WHY - Why did you decide to pursue this income generating idea?

> *e.g. I have sales expertise that can help new businesses gain traction. My grant writing background will help new nonprofits gain access to funding.*

WHAT – What specific services do you offer these customer groups? What is your value proposition? What are the key messages that define your value proposition to each group (try to narrow the focus to address pain points related to the industry or customer group)?

> *e.g. Commission based skin-care product sales services for startups; quality and quick copy editing services; grant application writing and review services; bookkeeping services.*

HOW – How will you reach each of your key customer groups? How will you inform them of the value you offer (identify the vehicles you will use)?

WHEN – If you need to volunteer some time to enable the target group to sample your value-add, when will this plan start generating income?

> *(e.g. With a couple of pressure cookers and a bag of seasoning in his car, Colonel Sanders cold-called on restaurants begging the owner to allow him to fry chicken for the employees. If they liked the chicken, the Colonel would stay a few days and cook for the restaurant's customers, with the understanding that a favorable reaction would be followed by franchise negotiations.)*

WHERE - Where would those groups most likely go to learn about products/services before making a purchase? Where will you find them online and offline?

Let's draft a plan to market your services to small businesses. Answer the questions on page 18:

WHO? Group 1	
WHY?	
WHAT?	
HOW?	
WHEN?	
WHERE?	

WHO? Group 2	
WHY?	
WHAT?	
HOW?	
WHEN?	
WHERE?	

WHO? Group 3	
WHY?	
WHAT?	
HOW?	
WHEN?	
WHERE?	

So, what did you learn about yourself in these first few pages? If you haven't learned anything yet – go back – get the pen or pencil in motion and complete the exercises!

What I learned: _____

_____

_____

_____

_____

_____

_____

_____

_____

_____

_____

_____

_____

Based on the exercises in this chapter and what you have learned, identify your next steps. For each action, identify the people and/or resources that can provide information, access to decision makers, ideas, or act as an accountability partner:

What actions do I need to take?	Partner(s)?	What will I ask them to do?

Chapter 2:

I Create for FUN!

Now is the time to have fun! The best part of creating what you love for this next life launch, is that the time you spend making additional money does not have to be stressful. There is an opportunity now to do what you have always dreamed of doing. Creating for fun will not only nourish your soul, but it can be spiritually uplifting too. Imagine being in harmony with your passions and the ability to freely create income based on your divine ideas.

A "new wave" of side jobs in the 21st century opens possibilities you couldn't have imagined in past decades. What if you just want to pick up some occasional work to save money for something special, like taking the grandchildren on a trip, joining a social club, or splurging on a trendy new wardrobe? How about some new camping gear, or season tickets to your favorite ballpark or performing arts center? There's a way to do those things now, without committing to set schedules or minimum wage drudgery. Here are a couple of real-life stories of Boomers who stowed away enough money for that special splurge by creating new opportunities to earn money that offer flexibility and creativity.

Creating for fun has nothing to do with paying the bills: it's all about sheer enjoyment!

Meet Jeanette & Corey

Driving for Dollars - Jeanette and her husband Corey both signed up as **ride-share drivers** for Uber in Orange County, California. Jeannette, as a natural "people person," accepted the first rider and chatted her way across town with a mechanical engineer on his way to an important meeting with county planners. She gained some valuable insight on the county's new light-rail plans – and pocketed enough money to start their piggybank fund for golfing in Scottsdale the following winter. Uber operates in hundreds of cities across the world, and states that independent Uber drivers make an average of $19 to $30 per hour, and sometimes even more if they're willing to drive during peak traffic hours or during major cultural events. Jeannette and Corey can pick up hours any time they like, with no commitments for when or how often they drive. They get paid weekly with direct bank deposits, or instantly via an Uber debit card. They'll be golfing in the sunshine next winter for sure! (Lyft drivers make up to $35 per hour. No car. No problem. Lfyt and Uber have car rental programs too).

Lyft has become a key component to my transportation strategy – as I decided not to bring a car to my new life in the Navy Yard (my monthly Lyft fees average $125/month – parking in my building is $200/month – *winning!*).

Meet Suzanne

Can you make a living working three hours a day? Suzanne dreamed of being a **travel writer** in her retirement years. After contacting magazines and newspapers in her Cincinnati home base, she realized that up to 90 percent of all travel writing nationwide is now doled out to freelancers. However, she needed some published writing samples to get the attention of editors and land a coveted travel writing assignment. That's when she discovered online content writing services such as Upwork, ZenContent, and Ebyline that hire writers to post blogs for major publishers and businesses. Regardless of the industry, most companies host blogs on their websites and need updated content. After signing up with a few writing services, Suzanne realized she could work whenever and wherever she chose – including on a beach in the Florida Keys! With careful planning, she earned enough to travel often and pay the expenses by writing for three hours a day.

Stuck? Here are a few ideas to get you started:

Travel much? If you love the outdoors, traveling, and discovering other cultures, and you want to meet people from different backgrounds – consider becoming a guide. What kind of guide? The key is to combine the things you are good at with the things you love to do. For example, if you have a talent for teaching and a love for fishing, consider becoming a fishing guide. Fishing, engaging with others, eating the bounty of your days' activity, sleeping under the stars on a fabulous fishing yacht – *I think you get the picture!*

It's me! My combination (talent + love) is: _____

Ideas to pursue: _____

_____

_____

Retired English teacher? Have you always dreamed of living in other countries and discovering the history, culture, and cuisine of places that are far away? Consider becoming an English as Second Language (ESL) teacher. There are many certificate programs that you can complete in a few months and apply for teaching jobs overseas (GOOGLE: Teach ESL abroad). Imagine teaching abroad for an entire year, traveling from one country to another while making money as you travel. Consider becoming a faculty member at Road Scholar: www.roadscholar.org.

It's me! My combination (talent + love) is: _____

Ideas to pursue: _____

_____

_____

Politically savvy with community ties? Consider engaging your community network and political talent to manage a candidate's campaign or another paid position – the work will be stimulating and the opportunity will most likely enhance your network.

It's me! My combination (talent + love) is: _____

Ideas to pursue: _____

_____

_____

Employment opportunities increase at hotels and resorts during high seasons. If winter is your favorite season, opt for a ski resort, or if summer is your favorite season, look for hotels by the beach or a lake. We talked about cruise ships before – explore it, if you love the sea. This is an opportunity to meet hundreds of people, travel the world, and enjoy all the fun activities offered by these leisure industries.

It's me! My combination (talent + love) is: _____

Ideas to pursue: _____

_____

_____

Nature lover? Consider a seasonal job at a national park. More people are needed during high seasons. You can commune with nature while providing needed service to others. How relaxing, motivating, and nourishing! Campgrounds may also offer seasonal opportunities (try https://www.nps.gov/aboutus/workwithus.htm).

It's me! My combination (talent + love) is: _____

Ideas to pursue: _____

_____

_____

Service-minded? The federal government hires people to assist when disasters occur around the country (consider: https://careers.fema.gov/ and watch for listings at http://usajobs.gov for opportunities with the Office of Disaster Assistance at http://sba.gov).

It's me! My combination (talent + love) is: _____

Ideas to pursue: _____

_____

_____

Golfer? Retired? Perfect combination, right? Consider working for a golf resort. This opportunity can include anything from being a ranger or driving the ball pickup machine. These resorts also have gift shops and restaurants. Create a living at a golf resort and play all the golf you can stand.

It's me! My combination (talent + love) is: _____

Ideas to pursue: _____

_____

_____

Now it's your turn!

What's your goal?	Cost?	When?	Three ideas to pursue:
Example: Going on a 9-day cruise.	$3,000	6 months	

The best part of creating a living to support fun and folly is that you can afford it ... that's what creating for fun means. This feeling alone will boost your confidence. Knowing you are having fun while engaging in your dream job, making money, and helping others while you improve your life connection is ultimately the goal of **creating for fun**.

What I learned: _____

_____

_____

_____

_____

_____

_____

_____

_____

_____

_____

_____

_____

_____

Based on the exercises in this chapter and what you have learned, identify your next steps. For each action, identify the people and/or resources that can provide information, access to decision makers, ideas, or act as an accountability partner:

What actions do I need to take?	Partner(s)?	What will I ask them to do?

Chapter 3:

I Create for the BASICS!

H ave you dipped your toe in the retirement pond and discovered that there are piranhas swimming in the waters? If you are in this group, survival is paramount, but that does not equate to desperation. Quite the contrary! Take a deep breath.

Some Boomers have found their monthly pension doesn't cover all possibilities, while others may find it is a struggle to meet their monthly expenses.

Although creating new ways of earning income is a solution many take, you still want to be able to have some down time to relax. After all, that is what this stage of life is all about. The last thing you want is to work a 50-hour week in a stressful environment which barely provides enough income to meet your monthly obligations.

Your options will depend on your needs:

Working to pay the rent. If you rent a house or an apartment, or have a mortgage to pay, then you will need enough income to cover this expense. Downsizing is also an option that will result in decreased housing costs, and moving may place you closer to your new job and reduce travel expenses or the need for a car. Now that I live in the Navy Yard, I have access to the metro (subway), DC Connector (bus line stops across the street), readily accessible Lyft and Uber (usually 2-3 minutes away), Car-to-Go, Maven and other 'hourly' car rentals are a stone's throw away. And of course, there's always good old-fashioned shoe leather (weight loss is a side-benefit).

Working to pay the utility bills. There's not much you can do about the cost of electricity, but the good thing is that utility companies usually have programs in place to help people manage the cost of their utility payments. Samuel in Seattle discovered that both Seattle City Light and Seattle Public Utilities offer a 50-60-percent discount for single customers with a gross monthly income of $2,600 or less (check with the utility as the requirements may change). On his retirement salary, he easily qualified for the program, automatically cutting his utility bills in half. Even those who don't qualify based on income can request to be put on a monthly "leveling" program that gages annual utility use and divides it evenly between 12 monthly bills, to avoid getting those surprise spikes for heating or air conditioning in the respective colder or hotter months.

Working to pay the food bills. After rent and utilities, food is probably the biggest expense you'll have. The number of people living in your household will determine how much you spend of course, but as you are retired (or considering it) it is safe to assume most households will consist of either one or two people. To help cover food costs consider becoming a "mystery shopper." While most jobs only pay between $7 to $20, many assignments are for restaurants and the company not only reimburses your meal but you make a few dollars too – you're essentially being paid to eat!

Meet Claire

Sometimes making ends meet means **thinking "outside the box"** in small ways that add up. When it comes to her food budget, Claire from Memphis decided to take stock of her minimal assets and skills to see if there was anything she could use to her advantage. She did have a decent sized yard (which cost a lot to mow in the summer, by the way). She devised a plan to put the yard to work *for* her instead of *against* her. After chatting with a handful of neighbors, the beginnings of a small community P-Patch emerged. Four neighbors helped prep the back portion of Claire's yard and sectioned off enough space to plant one vegetable each. In no time at all, three more neighbors joined, and the community garden grew to include fragrant herbs, tangled vines bursting with tomatoes, and enough summer squash to fill a deep freezer for the winter. Each person tended their own patch, meaning Claire wasn't stuck with all the work, and the bounty was shared by all, vastly reducing their grocery bills. To top it off, a few spouses took turns mowing Claire's lawn once a week during the growing season.

The Sharing Economy. Claire's story is a great example of how people are making money and/or saving money by sharing assets and resources. Jeanette and Corey (refer to page 24) also participate in this new "sharing economy" as Uber drivers sharing rides. Because of the Internet, people rent beds and homes, cars, boats, clothing and other assets directly from each other for a fee. Websites such as Airbnb, RelayRides, and Maven match owners with renters. Apps and social networks provide a way to order the service or schedule the rental; and online payment systems handle the billing.

Unique sharing sites include:

- www.spinlister.com: Rent ski, surfing and cycling equipment
- www.dogvacay.com: Sitters take care of your dog in their home
- www.thepeoplewhoshare.com: List sharing economy websites

According to a poll from TIME, strategic communications and global public relations firm Burson-Marsteller and the Aspen Institute Future of Work Initiative, 44% of U.S. adults have participated in such transactions, playing the roles of lenders and borrowers, drivers and riders, hosts and guests. [3] The sharing economy is not for everyone, but it could offer a unique way to earn money. As always, do your due diligence!

Working to pay other bills. As with every household there are often surprises: a bill to repair your car, a leak in the roof, an appliance in need of an overhaul. These unexpected expenses have the capacity to take a bite out of your monthly finances or savings. But by working just a few extra hours a month you can put enough aside to have a safety net when things go wrong.

Remind yourself that you are working so that you don't have to worry about that surprise bill, the increase in gas payments during winter, a two-week visit from your family, or attending a family reunion.

Clarity is key! Quantify your needs (develop a budget if you do not already have one to determine your financial goals):

I need to generate $ _____ /month.

Job Types that Might Work for You

Part-time jobs offer many benefits including the flexibility to enjoy traveling, dinner out, theater, and even volunteering. There are also many possibilities. If you are an engaging presenter, consider teaching at a community college. Look through the community college circulars in your area to see the types of classes that are being taught by people just like you. What kind of classes can you teach – yoga, accounting, charcoal drawing, wine tasting? When I started my business in 2001, I taught at a community college. You do not earn a lot of money, but you can create a network of people who are interested in your work. Think strategically. What is the opportunity beyond the class? Coaching? Consulting? When you engage in an activity that does not pay much, you must identify other sources of

---

[3] http://time.com/4169532/sharing-economy-poll/

compensation. For example, evaluations, letters of recommendation, and referrals are methods of being compensated for your work – as they become sources to leverage your expertise. Also, get in the habit of sending a press release to announce new work to create an online footprint of your expertise.

Contract Jobs — These jobs are short-term and might be project specific. They work well for anyone who wants to earn money but not commit to a full-time or long-term engagement. Example sites that feature contract jobs: Indeed.com, Careerbuilder.com, or Idealist.org.

Ideas to pursue: _____

_____

_____

Temp Jobs — Temp jobs are often on-call and many require that you are available on short notice. The benefit of a temp job is that you are not obligated to take every job that is presented to you. You can work as much or as little as you need without being obligated to a job or a contract. Here are a few websites to consider:

- www.rover.com – dog walking
- www.care.com – babysitting, elder care, variety of assignments
- www.taskrabbit.com – variety of assignments
- www.thebabysittingcompany.com – babysitting
- www.retirementjobs.com – general opportunities

Ideas to pursue: _____

_____

_____

Hobby Jobs — Hobby jobs are small businesses that you create from your favorite pastimes. Can you turn your passion into a business? Many people do. Companies such as Amazon have a handmade business model that allows you to sell your goods online. Facebook has the Shopify brand that offers an easy to create eCommerce website. Etsy has become the go-to website for artisans and crafters. Other options include craft fairs and placing products in local stores.

Ideas to pursue: _____

_____

_____

Consulting — With your extensive experience, skills, and expertise can you become a consultant? Can you create enough work that provides a solid income and the freedom to enjoy retirement? Yes, you can!

Ideas to pursue: _____

_____

_____

Coaching — Put your wisdom to work. Life and executive coaching can provide a lucrative income, but please consider obtaining certification. There are great programs that provide the methodology behind coaching, which is different from consulting. Consultants are hired to provide answers; coaches are hired to ask the right questions.

The options available to you depend on your requirements for income, willingness to be creative, and your drive to succeed.

Ideas to pursue: _____

_____

_____

Meet Deborah

I'd been here before, a place that I decided I would never return. My 50th birthday was fast approaching, and I had been laid off for the second time. I knew then that I would never again allow someone else to dictate my livelihood. As I contemplated what I would do to commemorate my birthday, I set aside the concern about finding employment knowing that I would land on my feet. I had a theme in mind for the celebration: "going back to my roots." I'm Jamaican. My parents moved to the United States when I was 6 years old. Although I had visited on occasion, I had never lived in Jamaica. So, my parents, my son, and a few friends rented a villa **and** spent a week in Jamaica to celebrate my dad's birthday as well as mine, which are two days apart. I had never felt so connected to a place. Walking out on a pier, as I gazed across the ocean, I decided that I would spend every birthday, from this day forward, on the island of my birth.

Even though I knew I was returning home to unemployment, I felt different. I had received a small severance from my job in the **quality improvement** industry and coupled with unemployment benefits, I could manage for a few months until I figured out my next steps. Every Saturday morning, I would ride my bike with a friend and his young son strapped to the back of his bike. Cycling was both a form of exercise and enjoyment; it was a much-needed stress release. At the time, I was riding a 1986 Club Fuji bike that I had paid $300 for back in the day. It was the best time of my life – I was happy, despite my employment situation. My bike, however, needed a tune up! A friend, who worked in a local bike shop, suggested that I purchase a new bike. But a decent bike was $1500-$1800 – such an investment felt irresponsible. So, he referred me to a Facebook site for used bikes. As I waited for my old, reliable bike to be tuned up I looked at the 'new for you' bikes. I came across an ad for a **186-mile cycle ride across the island of Jamaica**! I was immediately intrigued by the idea – then I glanced back at my old, reliable bike with gears that were down-shifters, and not on the handlebars. I really wanted to do it, but knew it would be improbable with *my ole girl*. The event was four weeks away. I'm the kind of person who once I get an idea, I do not stop until I achieve the goal or exhaust the idea. Two weeks later, I had a brand-new bike (courtesy of my 401(k)). I contacted **my local bike club, which is one of the largest cycling clubs in the US,** to help with my preparation and to become comfortable with my new bike. My first ride with the club was memorable; they took off and left me behind. How could I ride *185 miles?* I could not even ride one mile! I did not know how to work my gears and by the end of my first ride with the cycling enthusiasts, they did not have any confidence that I could make the 185-mile trek. With two weeks left, I rode a 3-mile bike trail at Hains Pointe every other day until I gained comfort with my new bike and confidence in my riding ability.

When we arrived in Montego Bay, I was anxious not to repeat my initial experience with the **members of the cycling club.** This time, there were 18 experienced riders and I did not want to be 'the one' who held up the group. The two weeks of practice paid off. I made it: 185 miles across the island of my birth! However, I did not *see* the island as my focus was on the gears, the mountains and at night, resting up for the next morning's ride. After the 3-day excursion was over, I stayed an extra week at a friend's vacation house who lived in Montego Bay. Every day, the guides from the island ride would pick me up at 6:00 AM to ride – I had ridden nearly 100 miles during the week and made friends with the guides. The night before my flight home, one of the guides asked me, "Why are you going home?" It wasn't like I had a job. But, I didn't have a place to stay as my friend had already rented out her house. They said, "No problem." So, my new friends found me a place to stay and I blissfully biked around the island with them for another week. During the week, Fowly, **the senior, most respected guide** began to confide in me and shared that his dream was to start his own bike touring business. Fowly and I spent most of the week talking about how this business might be developed. I went home in May and started living with the idea of a Jamaican cycling touring business. I spoke with friends and family and, through "What's App," kept in close communication with Fowly.

By June, I had sublet my apartment for the entire summer, shipped 10 bikes to Jamaica, made all the appropriate notifications and arrangements, bought an inexpensive ticket, packed up for 4 months, and moved to Jamaica just in time for my 51st birthday. I had started a business while fulfilling the promise that I made to myself to spend my birthdays on the island of my birth. During that 4 months, I learned an awful lot about setting up a business on the island. I learned just how much we take for granted in our fast-paced, Internet-driven business economy here in the United States. In Jamaica, it's different – starting with the use of carbon paper (I just took you back). I had not seen carbon paper in a very long time. In a way, I loved the experience – it was slow, but genuine. I had to learn the culture, especially with regards to how to conduct business in Jamaica, 'mon. I learned to be patient. It took 6 weeks to obtain our license to open **Super Fowl Cycling Tours, LLC** on the island of Jamaica. We are a concierge cycling company offering three services:

- Day tours: 3-hour tours from the guest hotel that includes stops along the way for food, mineral baths, and other attractions.

- Professional coaching and training for cycling clubs and teams. Fowly is a professional cyclist and member of the Jamaican Cyclist Federation.

- Super Fowl Century Tour: 5-days, 4-nights, 3-cycling days of majestic ocean views, and eco-bike friendly private accommodations nestled in the most tranquil parts of the island.

Deborah found a way to make a living while finding my bliss on the island of my birth.

For more information, visit: www.cyclingtoursjamaica.com

What I learned: _____

_____

_____

_____

_____

_____

_____

_____

_____

_____

_____

_____

Based on the exercises in this chapter and what you have learned, identify your next steps. For each action, identify the people and/or resources that can provide information, access to decision makers, ideas, or act as an accountability partner:

What actions do I need to take?	Partner(s)?	What will I ask them to do?

Chapter 4

I Create to Pay My Health Insurance

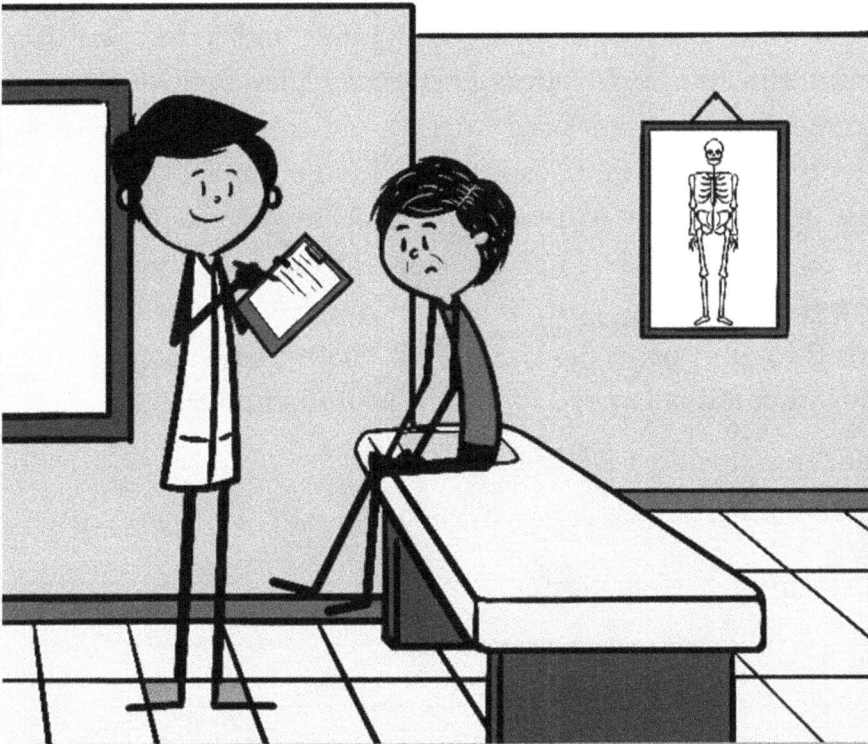

Some Boomers find themselves in a very difficult predicament – they have retirement funds to adequately support themselves, except for one major expense – *health care*. With the Medicare eligibility fixed at 65 for the foreseeable future, many Boomers have several months to several years to wait before they can enroll. As I am writing, health care policy is being debated. The unpredictability of current health care policies being discontinued or defunded is swirling around.

However, there are several health care options that can help you bridge the gap to Medicare (if the benefit remains in place), all of which are more accessible when you're generating income and working after retirement. Whether you work part-time in a retail store or explore some of the more creative options discussed in Chapter 5, extra income will make health care expenses less taxing to your budget until you reach Medicare eligibility. If you have not already identified your post-retirement cost, do your homework. Identify the costs that apply to you:

Employer Programs. If your employer offers a full healthcare benefit after retirement, consider yourself blessed and highly favored! If you're lucky, your former employer offers a healthcare plan that you can join even after retirement. While these programs are less common than they used to be, it's worth investigating, especially if you are still planning your retirement. However, these plans are typically expensive – with your employer no longer paying half or more of the premium, you may be responsible for the entire cost. Whether you pay for health care out of savings or through post-retirement work, these plans usually offer great coverage, and you'll only need to purchase until you reach 65.

Employer Programs Post-Retirement Cost:

_____

_____

_____

_____

COBRA. After you leave your employer's health plan, you'll have an opportunity to enroll in COBRA coverage. This plan offers short-term health insurance at a premium cost. You're limited to 18 months of coverage; you will need to pay the entire premium cost plus an administrative fee. While expensive over a short period, if you're close to Medicare age, it might be feasible to use extra savings or income to purchase coverage.

COBRA Fees:

_____

_____

_____

_____

Private Insurance. There are also several private insurance plans that you can purchase independently. While the Affordable Care Act (ACA) made buying private insurance accessible, it is unclear how long such options will be available. If you're interested in an ACA policy, visit your state government's website to learn more.

Private Insurance Premium/Deductible:

_____

_____

_____

_____

Short-Term Health Care Plans. If you have only a short gap between retirement, a short-term plan may be the option. These policies are limited in their coverage – they often don't cover routine checkups and screenings – but they can serve as prevention against major medical expenses in the short term. Such programs are subject to state laws and regulations, so you'll need to check with your state's health department for specific information about available options, time limits, and costs.

Short-Term Health Care Premium/Deductible:

_____

_____

_____

_____

State Medicaid Plans. Depending on your current income level, you may qualify for your state's Medicaid program. The rules and restrictions vary depending on the state, so check with your eligibility with your state health department or their website.

Medicaid Eligibility:

_____

_____

_____

_____

Part-Time Employment. If you're already thinking about a part-time job, finding a position that also offers benefits allows you to attack two birds with one stone. While a benefit-offering position may seem like a mirage in the desert of job hunting, an increasing number of employers offer benefits to their part-time employees to attract higher quality workers. Companies such as Whole Foods, Starbucks, and Lowe's offer such plans. Some Internet research can help you identify companies that provide part-time benefit options, allowing you to focus your job search more strategically.

With access to an employer-funded health plan, you have a powerful way to control and manage your health care costs, even if you have pre-existing conditions or rely on expensive medication. Furthermore, remaining in the workplace allows you the opportunity to maintain social connections outside the home, which can help ease the transition between full-time work and complete retirement. While many Boomers report feelings of loneliness and difficulty down-shifting, part-time employment can make this adjustment easier, all while helping you manage your budget and bide your time until you're eligible for Medicare.

Meet Sandra

Sandra found out the hard way, after she retired at 63, that the available health insurance plans to tide her over until she was eligible for Medicare were way out of her price range. Even though she was relatively healthy, the monthly premiums for her age bracket were prohibitive. That's when she discovered a **Health Savings Account**, commonly known as an HSA. Many people confuse these kinds of plans with similar employer-based ones, thinking individuals are not eligible. Anyone can contribute tax-free dollars into an HSA, which works as a medical savings account that can be used to pay for medical expenses. Coupled with a high-deductible health insurance policy that kicks in for major expenses and emergencies, the HSA provides a medical "slush fund" to pay for her co-pays, deductibles, and legitimate medical expenses. The best part is that the money contributed to the HSA rolls over every year if not used, so Sandra continues to have a growing health care savings account, and the money is all hers. Once she does qualify for Medicare, she can either leave the money in the account and continue to use it for medical bills, or she can withdraw any remaining funds and just pay the taxes she avoided paying when she deposited the money.

Whatever you choose, it is important you carefully consider your health care options after you retire. Going without coverage is not a viable option for most people, but finding a creative way to manage your health insurance costs and options until you reach Medicare age is easier than ever before. By planning in advance, you will be prepared for the additional costs short-term coverage might rack up and the limitations of these programs. But, importantly, you can also better target post-retirement employment opportunities that will help you meet your health care needs.

What I learned: _____

_____

_____

_____

_____

_____

_____

_____

_____

_____

_____

_____

_____

_____

_____

Based on the exercises in this chapter and what you have learned, identify your next steps. For each action, identify the people and/or resources that can provide information, access, ideas, or act as an accountability partner:

What actions do I need to take?	Partner(s)?	What will I ask them to do?

Chapter 5:

I Create on the Web

The WWW (World-Wide Web) is the best thing that has been invented since sliced bread! Working on the web provides flexibility and independence that many Boomers want to create for their next career. My business was created in 2001 as an "in the meantime activity." While looking for a six-figure job, I was told it might take 12-18 months to find the position that I desired. So, **in the meantime**, I created a consulting business to serve as a placeholder on my resume until I could find meaningful work.

As a solopreneur, the web has been my business partner, research team, classroom, and vehicle for advertising, as well as procuring and engaging with new clients. This book was illustrated, edited, reviewed, and sold through online resources. I've hired people and people have hired me through the web. The options for creating and re-creating are limitless, with both part-time and full-time opportunities, including freelancing.

Even more importantly for Boomers, conducting business on the web can be age-neutral.

eCommerce. In addition to freelancing, which made up 34% of the American workforce in 2016,[4] e-commerce businesses also allow you to earn extra income through online stores. For example, Etsy or Craftsy are online platforms to sell arts and crafts. Another popular platform, Shopify, provides a platform for customized stores that include marketing, shipping, and payment details. It also can be used as a plug-in, making it easy to add to your Etsy profile, your Amazon account, your Facebook page, or your personal website. Other e-commerce options include WordPress and its equally popular counterpart Wix. Both sites allow a user to link their e-commerce store directly to their website. An e-commerce business has the potential to earn money effortlessly, even while you sleep.

Ideas to pursue: _____

_____

_____

Job Seekers. Working on the web only requires an open mind and a bit of creativity. To find the best fit, you should first assess your interest and current skills set. For example, if you are a problem-solver and like interacting with others, consider applying for customer service positions. Some of the most common online jobs include:

- Medical coder
- Medical transcriptionist
- Insurance adjuster
- Writer

- Case manager
- Sales representative
- Account executive
- Administrative assistant

For more traditional opportunities, Monster.com, Careerbuilder.com, Indeed.com, and Idealist.com are two of the most popular general job boards, while other job boards are tailored to specific occupations. If you

---

4 Elaine Pofeldt, Forbes.com

are interested in working for the federal government, visit USAJobs.gov. Niche boards provide jobs related to specific industries, in addition to specific qualifications (bilingual), security clearance, and types of work (e.g. freelance, telecommute, contract).

Examples of niche job boards include:

- Crunchboard.com
- GitHub.com
- CharityChannel.com
- Chronicle of Philanthropy
- CADTalent.com
- ProjectManagementInstitute.com
- WriterAccess.com

Ideas to pursue: _____

_____

_____

Freelancers. If you want to have more autonomy, there are sites that cater to freelancers and short-term contract work. These sites include Fiverr, Freelance, People Per Hour, Thumbtack, and Upwork. Whereas on a job board like Indeed.com, your resume is the driver for a potential employer, on the freelance sites you create a profile that describes your services, name your price, and market your services. Most of these sites allow you to bid on jobs based on your profile and/or a job request posted by an "employer" (likely an entrepreneur like me in search of talent that enables expansion of my service offerings). Fees for entry level services can be low, but you can elevate earnings with enhanced services. People Per Hour and Upwork allow the freelancer to set an hourly rate. Skills that are usually marketed on these sites include:

- Web Design
- Graphic Design
- Writing
- Animation
- Social Media
- Marketing
- Advertising
- Music

But, you certainly are not limited to these standard categories. For example, Fiverr started as a site that promoted freelancers who would do anything (legal) for $5.00. Here are a few examples of "gigs" that are posted for sale (don't judge):

- *I will edit your video in my cool TUTTING dance. (King Tut)*
- *I will provide a message wearing a Unicorn head.*
- *I will create a video spilling a bottle of milk on my head.*
- *I will record a video of my cat reacting to anything you want.*

My point is – <u>anything is possible</u>, right?

Ideas to pursue: _____

_____

_____

Webinars and Online Courses. Another profitable way to create on the web is through webinars, better known as online courses. If you consider yourself an expert in a niche, you can package content to be sold to the masses. This option, by far, will require the most planning, creating, and marketing, but will result in the highest profit margin if done correctly. The size of your course participants is unlimited. You can create a short course to be taught through a series of emails, or you can create a comprehensive course that is self-taught. There are many platforms that will help you organize and provide your content to the public, including Udemy, Mind Flash, and Teachable.

Planning is an important aspect in creating a successful course. While you are creating the content, build an audience via blogging, social media engagement, or offering free content. This activity will also serve as your market research. Find out what people want or need to know about your topic. What are their pain points? Then, create a product that best suits their needs.

There are several resources that can help you build an audience and create buzz for the launch of your course; you don't have to reinvent the wheel. Learn from the masters! Attend webinars and online courses as part of your research. What did you like? What do you want to emulate? People like Neil Patel and Dorie Clark offer great, easy to understand content that can help you get started.

Online courses provide an unprecedented opportunity to share your knowledge with others, while sustaining the flexibility gained through retirement. The earning potential of an online course is only limited by your imagination and willingness to put in the time. While there may be many experts in your niche, your message and delivery of the content is unique, and that's what will sell it. So, my point is don't limit yourself – think outside the box – because there are opportunities to create and sell almost anything online. *(Remember the Pet Rock? And that was before the Internet).*

Ideas to pursue: _____

_____

_____

Meet Joseph

After retirement, Joseph found himself gravitating more and more toward one thing he'd always loved doing on his days off: treasure hunting at local thrift stores. With literally dozens of them scattered about his hometown of Minneapolis, he discovered that his "nickel and dime" habit was costing him some serious change every month. But it dawned on him one day that his biggest asset was his time; he was finding valuable things every day at pennies on the dollar because he had the *time* to spend roaming the aisles for gently used items that could be repurposed and *re-sold*!

Using the Internet, he started posting items that he'd found in thrift stores on eBay and Craigslist for up to five times the price he'd paid for them. Once, he even scooped up an old camera lens for $5 and sold it online for a whopping $225. It does take some patience to find the right buyer and to develop an eye for what will re-sell at a profit. But the great thing about this online "job" is that he still loves the thrill of "popping tags" (the slang term for thrift store rummaging).

A Word of Caution

While it is true that the opportunities are plentiful, it is also true that there are scams. There are phony companies that work to reel unsuspecting job seekers in with promises of making $5,000/month after a month of training. These scammers are usually trying to gain access to your personal information. **DO NOT GIVE ANY CONFIDENTIAL INFORMATION TO AN UNVERIFIED JOB OFFER.**

Do your due diligence. Research the company. Check them out with the Better Business Bureau. Check to see if they have a presence on LinkedIn (most legitimate companies are represented). Check out http://scambusters.org, http://scam-detector.com or http://scamwarners.com. The same advice that is applied to "prince charming," "the woman of your dreams," super car deals, and more applies here: **If it sounds too good to be true, it probably is.**

Here are some tell-tale signs of a scam:

- Vague job requirements and job description

- Unprofessional emails (e.g. typos, grammar mistakes)
- Emails that don't include contact information
- Online interviews via Yahoo Instant Messenger
- Request for training fees

The Internet is a powerful tool. Use it to your advantage. However, like everything else, be careful, and research companies before you give out your personal information. The main thing to remember when looking for work on the web is to protect your confidential information. Safety should be your number one priority. With these tools and an open mind, you will be working online in no time!

What I learned: _____

_____

_____

_____

_____

_____

_____

_____

_____

_____

_____

_____

_____

Based on the exercises in this chapter and what you have learned, identify your next steps. For each action, identify the people and/or resources that can provide information, access to decision makers, ideas, or act as an accountability partner:

What actions do I need to take?	Partner(s)?	What will I ask them to do?

Chapter 6

I Haven't Written a Resume Since 1999

Like many **Baby Boomers, you have retired after working for the same company for 10, 20, or 30 years.** Promotions were internal, and although you may have needed to apply for the new position, it did not require a resume. After all, most of the people on the selection panel either knew you personally, had heard of your good work, or respected the person who referred you.

The last time you were actively seeking work, Bill Clinton was president, The Matrix was at the movie theatre, and you were the proud owner of a Blackberry. *It's been a while!*

So, what is the best way to market yourself? You will still need a resume and here are some tips on how to improve it.

Your everyday routine for the past 20-30 years is now a memory (*Bam!* there it is — don't panic, just breathe). During that period, you made friends, you learned how to lead, you established a discipline (or expertise), and you inspired others to grow. For the last year or so you've travelled, joined the bridge club, the mall walking club and the book club and you've taken cooking classes, French classes, and auto repair classes. And, one day, while walking past the mirror – you took a glance and then a longer look – and discovered you want to go back to work.

Now where did I put that resume? For the first time in forever, you need a resume, but how do you condense everything you have done into one document? How can the lapse in time be accounted for between retirement and now?

Many questions swirl through your mind and before you know it, you are overwhelmed, confused, and not sure where to start. Don't panic! Lucky for you, I've engaged a resume expert to guide you through the re-invention of your resume. Please meet, Abby Locke (we'll affectionately refer to her as – you guessed it – *Dear Abby!*)

Dear Abby, can you provide a few strategies to help develop our professional resumes?

1. **Your resume is a strategic marketing document.** It should address your experience, skills, expertise, and achievements, but it is not a historical career document. You don't need to include everything you have done in your entire career. Depending on the position you are targeting, only include relevant and related career information.

2. **Your resume is not a one-size-fits-all document**. The layout, content, and strategy that worked for your best friend may not work for you. Start with the end goal in mind. With every piece of career information, ask yourself: "Will my future employer care about this?"

3. **Your resume on its own will not land you a new job**. Your resume is instrumental in opening the doors for interviews and creating connections that can lead to a new job. Therefore, it's very important to include your career achievements. Achievements demonstrate to your future employer how well you have performed and what your contributions have been to your past employers.

4. **Your resume's length should be proportionate to your career history.** Ignore the one-page resume myth. While you don't want to create a five- or six-page resume (unless you are targeting federal government positions), avoid squeezing all the great content from your career into one page.

5. **Your resume is best received (by employers and recruiters) when it's in chronological format even if you are changing careers.** I hate to say it but using a functional or skill-based resume format can create confusion for employers and hiring managers as it can be challenging to determine how your experience fits their needs. Use a combination format that highlights your relevant experience and transferable skills while keeping the main resume content in chronological order.

6. **Your resume and career background should be accessible to employers and hiring managers in both online and offline formats.** In addition to developing your resume in a Word document, you should create a LinkedIn profile (www.linkedin.com). Your resume should contain relevant keywords to increase the probability of being found by hiring managers conducting an online search. More than 80% of employers will do a Google search on your name and LinkedIn provides a common, easy-to-access to decision makers, and high-ranking tool for displaying your career information 24-7. You may also consider using a personal webpage/blog to demonstrate your skills set. LinkedIn is so important for your search, that you should consider taking an online class or read a book (look up: 'LinkedIn for Job Search').

NUTS and BOLTS Resume Preparation

Dear Abby, now that I've read the strategies, how do I dust off and update a resume that's been out of circulation for five to seven years?

<u>Six Easy Steps to Revitalize Your Resume</u>. With pen in hand – let's go to work!

STEP 1: Identify your career or job target

Your resume content will be influenced by your ideal job or career position. For example, if you are interested in working as a program manager, your resume should have details about your previous experience with program management, project leadership, team supervision, and other related skills.

In Chapter 1, you explored different opportunities to create this new adventure. If you are still unsure of your next career move, check out https://www.onetonline.org or https://mynextmove.org. These websites provide a wealth of information on different occupations, position requirements and even have assessments based on your skills and interests. Use online resources like www.linkedin.com, www.glassdoor.com and www.indeed.com to research available job opportunities that match your career background and/or your career interests at this stage in your life.

What is your job or career target?

_____

_____

_____

_____

_____

STEP 2: Create your ideal job profile

Once you have determined the type of job you want, it's important to get a better understanding about what employers are seeking in a candidate. More specifically, pay attention to the candidate requirements and qualifications of the job posting.

Questions to consider:

- How many years of experience are required?
- Do you need direct industry experience or can you train on the job?
- Is a college degree or advanced degree required?
- Are the jobs asking for industry or technology certifications?
- What level of technical proficiency is required (e.g. computer)?
- Does the job announcement list any industry specific software programs, systems or acronyms?
- Will you need to travel as part of the job?
- What key strengths are they seeking in a candidate (e.g. leadership experience)?
- Are the job-related tasks and position requirements familiar to you?

Use the chart below to compare existing job opportunities with your qualifications, expertise and background:

SKILLS, QUALIFICATIONS, EXPERTISE & EDUCATION REQUIRED	WHAT I BRING TO THE TABLE

STEP 3: Gather your career data/information

Often the most challenging aspects of developing your resume is remembering and finding all the career information you need for the project. The first place to start is pulling information from your old resumes and not just the most recent one. If your company was diligent about providing annual performance reviews, find your copies and focus on the ones from the last five to 10 years; if you don't have access to them, obtain a copy from the HR department.

Find your former position descriptions and copy the content from roles you held in the past 15 to 20 years. You can also use https://www.onetonline.org/ to find job descriptions for positions you held by searching by job title or similar titles. In addition, look for copies of certificates, awards, accolades or any special recognition you received over the course of your career.

Use a resume worksheet (see sample below) to compile all the details and information on your career background. Remember a good rule of thumb is to go back about 15 to 20 years; positions you held 25 and 30 years ago most likely are not relevant to today's working world especially in technology and computer proficiency.

Name: _____

Address: _____

City: _____**State:** _____**Zip:** _____

Home phone:_____ **Mobile phone:** _____

Email: _____ **LinkedIn URL:** _____

Career target: List top three job title choices in order of preference:

1. _____

2. _____

3. _____

Expected salary: _____

Education (list all degrees, certificates, diplomas received, dates received, schools or colleges, and location of schools or colleges). Please begin with the most recent and work backwards.

College/University: _____City/State: _____

Major: _____Degree: _____ Year _____

GPA: _____ *(if you remember or it was significant)*

Honors: _____

College/University: _____City/State: _____

Major: _____Degree: _____ Year _____

Training courses/seminars/workshops: (include names, dates, place, sponsoring organization)_____

_____

_____

_____

_____

Certifications _____

_____

Professional licenses: _____

_____

Professional organizations/affiliations: (include offices held) _____

_____

_____

_____

_____

_____

_____

Publications / presentations: title / periodical / location / date _____

_____

_____

_____

_____

Computer skills: (include hardware, operating systems, software, Internet, e-mail)_____

_____

_____

_____

_____

Foreign languages: (fluency — verbal/written)_____

_____

_____

Community activities (name of organization, years involved, positions held)_____

_____

_____

_____

Describe your work experience. Begin with present employer / project — include self-employment, volunteer or unpaid work if it applies. **List different positions at the same company as separate jobs.** (Note: if you are using someone to prepare your resume, copy this section and give it to them).

#1/Name of company: _____

City/State: _____

Dates of employment: _____

Your title or position: _____

Who do you report to (title)? _____

Number of people you supervised: _____

Your duties (briefly describe your duties, responsibilities, level of authority. Use numbers (size) and percentages, quantify budgets, state with whom you interacted): _____

_____

_____

_____

_____

#2/ Name of company: _____

City/State: _____

Dates of employment: _____

Your title or position: _____

Who do you report to (title)? _____

Number of people you supervised: _____

Your duties (briefly describe your duties, responsibilities, level of authority. Use numbers (size) and percentages, quantify budgets, state with whom you interacted): _____

_____

_____

_____

_____

#3/ Name of company: _____

City/State: _____

Dates of employment: _____

Your title or position: _____

Who do you report to (title)? _____

Number of people you supervised: _____

Your duties (briefly describe your duties, responsibilities, level of authority. Use numbers (size) and percentages, quantify budgets, state with whom you interacted, etc.):_____

_____

_____

_____

_____

STEP 4: Write your career achievement statements

At this point, you should have completed a considerable amount of work in chronicling your career and putting as much detail as possible into one worksheet for easy reference. Write your career achievement statements so that your resume has a good balance between your job tasks (what you were paid to do) and your achievements (how well you did your job).

Never doubt your value and think you don't have significant achievements. A career achievement is a benefit or an improvement that came as a direct result of your efforts or involvement. For example, if you were a sales manager in the past, some of your career achievements could be:

- *Grew revenues 15% by landing the largest account in the Mid-Atlantic region.*
- *Increased company's market share in highly competitive region by developing first-of-its-kind marketing strategy and tactical plans.*

Now don't worry if career achievements like these don't automatically pop into your head and roll off your tongue. Remembering every significant thing you have done in your career can be very challenging, so take it one step at a time.

First, start with your latest or most recent position and reflect on what it was like when you first took on the role. Did the company have a new initiative in place? Was the company going after a new client? Did the company just establish a new revenue goal? What was important and critical at that time?

_____

_____

_____

Second, look at your performance reviews during that job tenure and pull out all the career achievements and awards (individual or team based). If you don't have access to performance reviews, reach out to former colleagues and managers and brainstorm together about some of your big career achievements.

_____

_____

_____

Third, use memory-jogging questions to recall any career achievements you may have overlooked. The questions below will help you identify your achievements over the years (quantify the results when possible):

1. Did you identify and solve a problem for your department, manager or the company? What were the results?

_____

_____

_____

_____

2. Did you design or implement a process or procedure to make a job more efficient, easier or more accurate?

_____

_____

_____

_____

3. Did you help the company save money or time? By how much?

_____

_____

_____

_____

4. Did you increase productivity or reduce downtime? By how much?

_____

_____

_____

_____

5. Did you consistently exceed goals or objectives on certain projects or tasks? What were they?

_____

_____

_____

_____

6. Did you effectively manage systems or people? What were the results of your efforts?

_____

_____

_____

_____

7. Did you work between departments? What was your contribution?

_____

_____

_____

_____

8. What success did you have training or coaching individuals or a team?

_____

_____

_____

_____

9. Did you receive any awards, bonuses or promotions? What specifically did you do to get them?

_____

_____

_____

_____

10. What ways did you contribute to key decision making or planning?

_____

_____

_____

_____

11. Did you improve the efficiency of people or operations? What were the savings?

_____

_____

_____

_____

12. Were you responsible for reducing costs of an operation?

_____

_____

_____

_____

13. Were you involved in a company/department start-up, shutdown or reorganization?

_____

_____

_____

_____

14. Did you produce reports or data that enabled management to make more informed decisions?

_____

_____

_____

_____

Refer to the list on page 41 and identify your achievements:

1.	11.
2.	12.
3.	13.
4.	14.
5.	15.
6.	16.
7.	17.
8.	18.
9.	19.
10.	20.

STEP 5: Develop your summary of qualifications / profile

Your resume is your personal marketing tool, and the product you are selling is YOU. At first glance, especially in the profile / summary of qualifications section, you want employers and hiring managers to immediately know who you are, the value you bring to the table, and what **differentiates** you from other candidates.

The summary of qualifications or resume profile is the section that appears after your name and contact information. This section can include some or all of the following:

- An accomplishment or recognition.

- Top skills, talents or special knowledge.

- Something about your personal work style.

- Education, training, or certification.

Here are some examples of what a good resume profile should look like:

- *Versatile skill set with experience in customer service, sales, and business development. Earned multiple customer service excellence awards and possesses highly recognized mentoring and team leadership strengths. (Good for career changers).*

- *Performance-driven finance executive with deep expertise in spearheading initiatives that strengthens internal infrastructure, expands revenue-generating capabilities, and maximizes ROI for high-growth companies. (Good for transitioning to consulting roles).*

- *Results-driven professional with extensive customer service management experience. Exceptional leadership skills coupled with certifications in employee mediation and teambuilding. Innovative problem solver with history of implementing new processes that tripled customer satisfaction ratings. (Good for management roles).*

STEP 6: Bring it all together to form your new resume

Before you open a new Word file and dump everything into it, let's look at the most common sections of a professional resume. Decide what sections you want to use in your resume and remember to leave out irrelevant content your future employers don't need to see.

- Name / address / contact information (remember email and LinkedIn profile URL)
- Summary of qualifications
- Professional experience (including relevant volunteer and part-time work)
- Education, certifications and training
- Computer / technology proficiency
- Professional interests and special skills
- Special recognition and awards
- Community organizations / professional affiliations
- Publications and speaking engagements

Success tips for your new resume

<u>When finding keywords, industry jargon and relevant content:</u>

- Be diligent and consistent in your research so you can find the right language and keywords to include on your new resume:
  - Scour top aggregator job sites like www.indeed.com and www.simplyhired.com

  - Visit www.glassdoor.com to find top employers and visit the company websites

  - Leverage the best of the Occupational Outlook Handbook (https://www.bls.gov/ooh/)

  - Talk to other Boomers who have landed jobs or work with a career coach

  - Conduct informational interviews with professionals in your target field

<u>When writing your job tasks and career achievements</u>:

- Choose a few sentences that capture your skills, duties, and accomplishments.
- Don't limit yourself to paid work – reference leadership experience from volunteer assignments.
- Use action verbs/keywords in your writing; reference www.thesaurus.com for a variety of descriptive words.
- Include the results you achieved and the actions you took in reaching your goal. For example, *"Exceeded fundraising goal by 20% by effectively coordinating five events for breast cancer walk.*

<u>When writing your education / training</u>:

- If you completed training, list the certificate(s) you earned that are relevant to your target jobs.
- List college degree and advanced degrees on your resume including major/subject focus and relevant courses.
- If you do not have a college degree, list your high school degree and any other technical training programs or certificates.

That was a lot. *Right?* Take a deep cleansing breath and take a time out. Do you remember what a time out means?

Let's consider a few other ideas. The following tips will enable you to market your services in the 21st Century.

1) Build a Network

Lou Adler, CEO of a HR consulting firm, asked more than 3,000 people in staff or management roles during a 12-month period how they found their most recent job. He identified three types of job seekers: employed passive seekers, employed casual seekers, employed active seekers, and unemployed or under-employed active seekers. The following identifies the percentage of jobs found by networking:

- 62%: Employed passive seekers
- 60%: Employed casual seekers
- 42%: Employed active seekers
- 40%: Unemployed or under-employed active seekers

By the time jobs are posted online, either an internal candidate was not found or a referral from a trusted source does not exist. As you can imagine, it is much more expensive to conduct an external search for candidates than hire from within the organization.

Networking in your quest to seek employment does not mean telling everyone you meet you are looking for work. Instead, aim to engage a few well-connected people who know about your work can refer you to other networks of people. Make a list of the people in your warm network and share your capabilities and interests.

The following are a few tips adapted from Marlene Chism's Networking Builders:

- Networking is more than idle conversation or collecting business cards. Networking is building relationships and becoming a resource to others.
- Join organizations and associations that will allow you to demonstrate your skills by working on committees, programs and/or projects.
- Identify specific people that you want to meet in your professional association or chamber of commerce (refer to the membership roster). Do your homework before you meet. What do you have in common? Why do you want to meet him or her? How can you help? What do you have to offer?
- Make sure you have nicely-developed business cards that, at a minimum, provide contact information. List the three or four top skills you have someone might hire you for, but do not preface it with, "Looking for work".
- Create a list of networking vehicles (e.g. church, school, social events, meetups) where you can build relationships and/or share resources.
- When meeting someone for the first time, focus your effort on learning about the other person.

2) Utilize Social Media Platforms

You cannot rule out the value of social media in your quest to land a job. Job vacancies are posted daily on social media platforms so don't just consider them as somewhere to post updates or market products and services. You can equally stumble on posts (or comments) where an individual may indicate their need for a service you offer (as a freelancer). It is important to request testimonials on sites like LinkedIn as this is how some employers determine whether a candidate is viable.

LinkedIn is a network of 400 million people who are actively in networking mode. For those on the hiring side the reverse is true. With LinkedIn Recruiter you can search on your first-degree connection's connections (second level connection), rather than just asking who's the best person they know doing a particular job it's important to also ask about specific people you've found connected to them. LinkedIn is a critical resource. If you are not connected or building your network by contributing value, then you're missing one of the most important professional resources to help expand your thinking and engagement. It's not Facebook; it's strategic, deliberate and valuable!

Utilize LinkedIn or a personal website or blog to demonstrate your ability to do the work by providing a sample of your work (e.g. a slide show), or periodic blogging on a subject that highlights your expertise. Or, if you are an artist, display your work on websites (your personal site, LinkedIn, Facebook, and other niche sites) or create greeting cards with your artwork (worked for Zelda Wisdom). There are thousands of ways to attract your target audience; the key is to provide evidence of your specific skills and abilities.

3) Speak Up with Confidence

Never be afraid to tell others you want a job but do not act like your whole life depends on it. Simply say you want to provide a service. For example, if you are a chef looking for an opportunity, let people know about your catering services – even better, offer to cater an event where decision makers are present. Be prepared to talk about the benefits of using your services.

4) Engage

Sometimes you need to stand in the way of opportunity. In your quest to get a job, volunteer, volunteer, volunteer! Volunteering will expand your network. So, consider volunteering in organizations that will enhance your skill set, or within industries that you want to work. Also, consider volunteering with organizations that have a national presence, for example AARP Foundation Experience Corps, an intergenerational tutoring program that engages adults aged 50 and older to help children read at grade level with the goal of disrupting the cycle of poverty.

The other side of engagement is creating your own "board of directors" – people you can bounce ideas off. They are people who know you well and whose opinion you value. Ask them if you can include them on your team of "brand builders" or support team (however you want to phrase it), provide a purpose for what you want them to do – be specific, and an idea of how much of their time you are requesting.

5) To Dye or not to Dye: Image Opportunities

Let's be clear, ageism is alive and well. Although hiring managers can't (legally) ask you questions about your age, they can guesstimate from your resume and work history. You must take control of your appearance. People form opinions of you – right or wrong – within moments of meeting you. That means you can't afford to leave someone's impression of you up to chance. We all know snap judgments can be wrong and unfair. Still, you can't ignore the reality: people form opinions based on the most minor details.

People do judge books by their covers, every day. Make sure that your cover conveys the message you want people to remember. First and foremost, if you purchased your interview suit in the 1990s … think about an upgrade. Like it or not, a dated appearance does give the impression that your skills may also be dated. Your clothing, eyewear, and hair must tell the story that you are current. *That does not mean you should dress like a youngster*, but you must appear up-to-date, interesting, fresh, competent, etc. Invest in an all-weather wool suit in navy blue, charcoal gray or a muted color. For creative industries, you have more latitude with suit color. Then, make a statement about your personality with your scarf or tie choice and/or jewelry selection.

If your hair is silver, wear accents of blue or a French blue shirt to add vitality to your face. Depending on your personal coloring, a white shirt can drain the color from your face, leaving a "ghastly" appearance. If you have stark silver in your hair and the rest of your hair is black or very deep brown, avoid wearing brown tones as the color will make your hair look dull. *What about a dye job?* Yes, if you can get a professional to dye and maintain the look. Avoid stark colors, i.e. jet black at 62 years old. Use colors that look natural including a little silver around the temples. Aim for a look that connotes vibrancy, vitality and health ... that does not necessarily require a dye job.

A few minutes before your interview, use eye drops. Not only does it get the "red out," it also whitens and adds a little sparkle to your eyes. If your teeth are stained, consider professional teeth cleaning and/or whitening. Too expensive? Opt for an over-the-counter toothpaste with whitener.

Engage your board of directors (preferably younger members) to give you an honest opinion on your appearance and interview outfit. Don't create obstacles for yourself that can be easily addressed by a few minor changes!

That was a lot of information!

What I learned: _____

_____

_____

_____

_____

_____

_____

_____

_____

_____

_____

_____

Based on the exercises in this chapter and what you have learned, identify your next steps. For each action, identify the people and/or resources that can provide information, access to decision makers, ideas, or act as an accountability partner:

What actions do I need to take?	Partner(s)?	What will I ask them to do?

Chapter 7

I'm Not Too Old to Learn Something New!

T**ell the truth** ... *when was the last time you took a class? What was the class about? Was it enjoyable? Was it a class that you <u>had</u> to take or was it something that you <u>wanted</u> to take? Were you excited to learn something new?*

The reality is if you have been engaged in the same work for more than a few years, there are likely new ways to approach your work. If there is one defining feature of the modern marketplace, it is its rapid pace of change. It's important to stay current as laws, consumer expectations, business practices, and technologies are continuously in flux, requiring a constantly shifting set of skills. Alternatively, you may want to take a step in a new direction and learn new skills to jumpstart your perennial career. Although the pace of change is daunting, it's easier to adapt to than you may think. By taking advantage of new learning methods and drawing skills from your existing hobbies and interests, you can accrue all the skills you need to continue or start a vibrant career.

My Mom and Aunt

I am constantly inspired by my mother – she's my heroine for many reasons. My mom and aunt (who are twins) retired at the age of 51 from the City of Detroit. Mom worked for the Detroit Police Department as a civilian and my aunt for the Receiving Hospital. Soon

Mom's Bitmoji©

after retirement, they moved to Tacoma, WA where my uncle (their brother) has lived for decades.

Today, my mom and aunt are 85 years young. When they were 84 years of age, they both purchased an iPhone 6 and joined the communication age. They disconnected their landline – *I need to catch up to them!* Their response time on iPhone is within minutes (if not seconds). I nearly fell on the floor the first time these two adorable seniors Facetimed me – one was driving while the other held the phone. They talk, text, and even have Bitmojis. Months later, after my nephew asked a question, I laughed with great amusement when Mom texted back, 'Google it' – *(drop the mike!)*

My point is you are never too old to learn and embrace technology. *So, don't use age as a reason for not staying current.*

Making Use of Flexible Learning Methods

Although sitting in a classroom and learning from others has many advantages, including social aspects and networking, the world of education is at your fingertips thanks to modern technology. These methods provide affordable and accessible opportunities for learning. The most effective learning methods include:

- **Tutorial Websites** - A growing number of websites offer educational materials, allowing you to study a topic in depth for free or for a small subscription fee:

  - <u>Duolingo</u>, for example, provides free language training activities that are comparable to university courses. More than 20 languages are available from Spanish to Swahili and everything in between. I'm obsessed with this idea! For as little as five minutes a day, learn a new language.

  - <u>Codecademy</u> publishes courses in Java, Python, PHP, Sass, HTML, and a variety of other programming and markup languages. I'm not so obsessed with this one but, if you are interested in website development, this could be the perfect opportunity for you. You can learn to code for free. I

  - <u>Khan Academy</u>, another freebie, provides education on a myriad of topics: art history, math, grammar, chemistry and physics.

  - <u>Coursera</u> provides university courses that enable you to earn a certificate in four to six weeks. These and other websites offer marketable skills that any employer will value, or that will enable you to strengthen skills needed for freelancing or starting a business.

- **Educational Apps** – With mobile apps, you can study from almost any location, allowing you to incorporate your education throughout your life. Some apps help you to prepare for professional exams and certifications, while others directly teach you the skills that you will need. Some apps effectively make games out of their courses, motivating you to learn at every opportunity. Most apps have a small fee that supports the independent app designer. My favorites include:

  - EasyBib which functions as a basic citation generator for writers. It allows you to automatically create and export citations in a matter of seconds.

- The TED app provides the entire library of TED Talks videos, introducing you to intriguing presentations and revolutionary ideas.

- **Videos & Podcasts** - YouTube, Vimeo, and other online video sites provide access to lectures and webinars, many of them taught by university professors or experienced professionals. You can also download podcasts on educational topics and watch or listen to them while cooking, exercising, or performing other tasks during your day, allowing you to absorb new information without taking time away from other activities.

- **Research Tools** - If your field requires you to conduct your own research, digital databases offer unprecedented opportunities to do so. Services like JStor and Academia.edu provide instant access to peer-reviewed publications written by millions of people across the world for free.

Besides making learning easier, these methods also allow you to explore different fields of study. By using a wide variety of sites, apps, and learning tools, you can get a sense of what fields interest you the most and enjoy your ongoing education.

Learning Through Hobbies

The most effective way to learn new skills is to look for educational opportunities that already exist in your life and take full advantage of them. You already have enormous potential to learn. These are examples of how you can learn from your hobbies.

- **Learn From Your Website** - Programming, markup languages, and search engine optimization are all of immense value to employers. A website gives you the chance to hone these skills – and many are free (check out Wix.com). If you want to work in marketing, for example, experiment with new keywords, writing styles, and organizational techniques, determining how these factors affect your site's ranking. If you are learning programming or markup languages, practice them by writing new features for your site.

- **Love to Travel** - Traveling to other countries, or even to culturally diverse areas of your own country, allows you to immerse yourself in new languages and cultures. Given how many firms must do business across cultural and national boundaries, being multilingual is an invaluable skill. Thus, when you travel, use as little English as possible, taking every opportunity to learn new vocabulary and practice your pronunciation.

- **Interest in Mechanics** - If you have a car, motorcycle, or other vehicle that needs frequent repairs, consider making those repairs yourself. The same goes for appliances, electronics, and all other devices that allow you to practice mechanical maintenance skills. Just make sure to take proper safety precautions before working with potentially dangerous equipment.

What can you learn from your hobbies?

My hobbies	What can you learn from your hobby?

Learning through your hobbies doesn't just teach you skills, it also helps you to enjoy those activities more. Seeking knowledge in all you do is thus as important for your quality of life as it is for your ability to create.

What I learned: _____

_____

_____

_____

_____

_____

_____

_____

_____

_____

_____

_____

Based on the exercises in this chapter and what you have learned, identify your next steps. For each action, identify the people and/or resources that can provide information, access to decision makers, ideas, or act as an accountability partner:

What actions do I need to take?	Partner(s)?	What will I ask them to do?

In Conclusion

I've said enough. This is your journey and you must write the conclusion to this action guide. Review your responses to the exercises. Now, it's time to prioritize all the information that you have synthesized. What are you willing to do **within the course of a week** to powerfully move in the direction of creating new income opportunities that you jump out of bed to pursue? *Tall order?* I understand … but we are the generation that created words like 'groovy' and 'far out' as a way of expressing our sheer delight.

You have the creativity and drive to create something new and groovy, special, and far out for this next phase of life. **What is it?**

MY PRIORITIES

Review all your completed exercises. Identify your top five ideas or areas of interest:

1.	
2.	
3.	
4.	
5.	

PROMISE YOURSELF that you will use this action guide for **7 days**. Acknowledge all the actions that you complete – either by entering a date or a simple check mark in the COMPLETED column. Whatever actions you don't complete on the indicated day should be considered the next day, unless you find that these actions are no longer required.

Your 7-Day Action Plan

DAY 1			
WHAT?	WHEN?	WHERE?	COMPLETED?

DAY 2			
WHAT?	WHEN?	WHERE?	COMPLETED?

DAY 3			
WHAT?	WHEN?	WHERE?	COMPLETED?

DAY 4			
WHAT?	WHEN?	WHERE?	COMPLETED?

DAY 5			
WHAT?	WHEN?	WHERE?	COMPLETED?

DAY 6			
WHAT?	WHEN?	WHERE?	COMPLETED?

DAY 7			
WHAT?	WHEN?	WHERE?	COMPLETED?

Congratulations, on finishing your 7-day action plan. Now let the universe work with you to attract the opportunities to you. But, don't let the plan gather dust! If there's no activity, shift gears and review your priority list…then, get back in action!

Funny thing, if you are working towards your goal with enthusiasm, an open mind and a spirit of adventure, you are certain to manifest a great opportunity.

You're a part of the perennial workforce. Just like any other perennial, water the seeds of opportunity that you have planted and nurture them as they grow.

References

Foreword

A retirement mind map is a specific version of a "vision page." It is a collection of images, words, and photos that represent the things you want to have, be, or do in your life. Marcia used PowerPoint and found logos and photos online to create her mind map. Or, you can create a vision board using a variety of magazines, double-sided photo tape, and scrapbook paper or card stock.

Seven easy steps for making a "vision page"

By Carla Dancy Smith

1. Write a list of goals that you'd like to achieve.
2. Find pictures that depict your goals and clip pictures with your heart, not your head.
3. Create a collage out of all these images and affix to a scrapbook page or cardstock using the double sided-photo tape.
4. Be inspired to make one page for your vision or a page for each area of focus (similar to Marcia's four quadrants).
5. Include pictures of yourself in the collage. See yourself in the vision. Be creative and provocative.
6. Clip motivational affirmation words or phrases and inspiring quotes that speak to you and how you want to FEEL, like "courage," "love," or "imagination."
7. Place your vision board where you can see it – first thing in the morning and last thing at night. Sign and date the back of the page.

Chapter 1

Colonel Sanders:
http://www.newyorker.com/magazine/1970/02/14/kentucky-fried

Leo and Lillian Goodwin:
https://www.geico.com/about/corporate/history-the-full-story/

Carol Gardner: http://zeldawisdom.com/about.shtml

Chapter 3

https://www.economist.com/news/leaders/21573104-internet-everything-hire-rise-sharing-economy

https://www.forbes.com/sites/bernardmarr/2016/10/21/the-sharing-economy-what-it-is-examples-and-how-big-data-platforms-and-algorithms-fuel/#d76abcc7c5af

Chapter 4

http://www.moneycrashers.com/part-time-jobs-health-insurance-benefits/

https://www.hhs.gov/answers/medicare-and-medicaid/who-is-eligible-for-medicaid/index.html

https://www.dol.gov/agencies/ebsa/about-ebsa/our-activities/resource-center/faqs/cobra-continuation-health-coverage-compliance

http://money.usnews.com/money/retirement/articles/2011/05/02/how-to-get-retiree-health-insurance-before-65

Chapter 7

http://static.duolingo.com/s3/DuolingoReport_Final.pdf

https://www.livecareer.com/quintessential/portfolio-careers

https://about.coursera.org

https://www.khanacademy.org

https://www.codecademy.com

https://www.safaribooksonline.com

Credits

Illustrator: Galih Winduadi
Editors: FirstEditing.com
Book Designer: Samuel Okike

He fills my life with good things, so that I stay young and strong like an eagle.
Psalm 103:5 (GNT)

www.ingramcontent.com/pod-product-compliance
Lightning Source LLC
Chambersburg PA
CBHW081133090426
42737CB00018B/3319